Alchemy of the Soul

A Love Story of the Heart and Mind

Stacy L. Pintor

GLASSSPIDERPUBLISHING

To all of us finding our way home.

To my sacred self for lighting the way to the union of my heart and mind, the divine feminine and masculine within, one of the greatest love stories I've experienced and continue to experience.

To Rhea, my beloved daughter, for traveling on this chariot with me.

To my soul family for holding a loving space, even when you didn't always understand my path.

Contents

Preface

Welcome into a glimpse of my soul. In these pages, a love story of the heart and mind, the long-awaited union of the divine feminine and masculine within, will unfold in poetic verses. I "bare my soul" in these poems as an example of soul alchemy, healing, growth, and expansion. My poetry is introspective and transcendental as I explore the deep crevices of the heart and mind, only to find a sweet connection with my inner knowing and wisdom that always lights the way and guides me to alignment with my sacred self.

For a long time, I sought happiness, abundance, security, and safety from the external world. But for me, it was all taken in an instant with the tragic loss of my beloved soulmate almost twenty years ago. It was then that I realized how seeking from the outside can be fleeting, unfulfilling, even devastating. I knew I needed to build from within so no external change could ever take from me again.

I also knew building from within meant cleaning house. Clearing and purging my mind and heart of any preconditioning that was holding my creation hostage or discouraging the full expression of my sacred self. I knew I could not fully align with abundance, opulence, affluence, and joy while still making space for a heavy and dense load of mental and emotional clutter and burdens. I marched forward with a deep sense of perseverance to clean my internal space. This collection of poems is a direct reflection of that determination. As you will find, the clutter illuminated my attachment to lack and fear: a lack of feeling supported, a lack of fulfillment in career changes, a lack of a partner, a lack in finances, and the fear of a new way of existing and thriving.

Once the space was cleared and purged, I felt quite anxious, and the temptation to once again get entangled in my mental stress was persistent. I wanted to hastily fill the empty space I'd created, but my sacred self prevented such haste.

My sacred self significantly slowed my creation down to a point of a standstill. This time of stillness (which at times felt more like an unwanted delay) forced me deeper within. It led me to a place of surrender and acceptance, of aligning with peace and harmony, out of complete mental exhaustion and burnout. I was aligning more and more with my heart and sacred self, but my addiction to mental stress was still present. However, the grip it had upon my existence was getting less and less intense, and so I was able to have some altitude with the stress. I saw it for what it was: an experience of the soul. In this collection, you will also witness this altitude and the sweet reunion with my sacred self as this connection develops and becomes stronger in each poem.

After some time within, the reason for the slowing became crystal clear to me. I had to prepare the newly cleared space with an energy of complete harmony, peace, calm, and balance before higher vibrational manifestations could enter the space. If I hastily filled it, I would have filled it with more of the same: lack and fear. This is where I am now, sitting in the center of an open, cleared space drenched with sunlight and warmth, and feeling a profound sense of peace and harmony. I know from here I will begin filling the space with all that resonates with this foundation of harmony, and the new will flow in with ease and grace. The "new" has always been there but was hidden behind the veil of fear and lack.

A major aspect of the divine masculine also became clear to me. The divine masculine supports and protects the divine feminine's creation—a simple understanding, but the fullness and the essence of this revelation resonated to the core of my being. As I sit in this space of complete peace and harmony, I will be able to fully receive the divine masculine's protection and support of the divine feminine's expansive creation all from within and without.

Included at the end of each poem is the meaning of the poem. I know at times I have read poetry and wasn't clear on the meaning even though I really desired to know, and so I offer you my meaning. However, the poems are entirely open to your interpretation, your meaning, and your resonance with each. I'm just hoping these poems do resonate with you and inspire you to be a poet of your own healing, growth, and expansion.

At the end of the book, you will find a special treat. It is a poem written by my daughter. She is an extraordinary divine gift to me, an old soul here to share her wisdom.

I hope you enjoy this love story!

—Stacy L. Pintor

The Love Story Begins…

Critique

Why am I here?
In this space that professes to help me to expand,
to refine my craft.

I keep wanting a break
for someone to acknowledge me:
celebrate me
love me
accept me,
the unrelenting desire for acceptance.

Don't critique me,
you are hurting me.
Don't you know how great I am?
I am amazing just as I am.
You may not resonate with me,
see my brilliance,
perhaps, you don't understand my language.

Is it for me to clarify,
to make more concrete, as you say?
Once again, I'm asked to restrict my truth.

I've worked diligently to be abstract, creative,
to go beyond my boundaries,
expand into the ether.

It's for you,
to find your own meaning.
I know my meaning,
thanks to your critique.

---

*Critique is about the journey of creation, which means the
inevitable critique that comes along for the ride, both internally
and externally. I used to have a hard time receiving any criticism
because it illuminated self-limiting beliefs that were still lurking
in my psyche. I've come to realize, though, that this light provides
an opportunity to restore empowerment. The poem describes my
experience when I attended a poetry workshop, which helped to
reaffirm my faith and belief in my writing and its potential.*

The Deep Unknown

Soft
are the faint whispers of the deep unknown,
calling me towards it.
Apprehension consumes me
as I contemplate traversing its edges,
let alone its core.

Tip toe
around its rim, each step placed carefully.
A hint of cautious impulsivity dares me
to dip one toe in,
a coolness ascends through me,
a flutter of breath, shivers of curiosity,
somehow inviting.

Hesitation
dip the other toe in to find the same,
a persistent allure to plunge, to let go.

Ponder
dive in or gradually descend?
Oh, what the hell!

Leap
with arms extended in a sacred posture
of full acceptance, unyielding faith.
Falling
no need to panic,
feeling held and supported, safe.
Descending
into darkness, plunging deeper and deeper,
trusting the journey.

Halt
suspended in darkness, cradled,
gently swaying in the unknown's embrace, resting.
Until an electric jolt, a golden beam of light
traverses my entire being,
a burst of power and confidence
blazes through me like a flamed arrow.
My posture immediately straightened
with strength and fortitude;
I am aligned.

Break
the curtain of darkness pulls back,
revealing a glorious light, luminous and radiant.
Blinding at first sight, covering my eyes,

drawn to look again
to find complete visual bliss,
only I can see.

Alive
breath flows deep, with ease and grace
replenishing my lungs with truth and wisdom,
emanating authenticity.

Ascend
from the depths of the deep unknown
into the light, my light.

---

*The Deep Unknown describes the fear of the unknown, whether
it is within or outside of us. It's about relating to the unknown in
a different way than with trepidation and avoidance. The poem
suggests shifting your perspective of the unknown, which can
lead to a feeling of empowerment. In this poem, I venture into the
deep unknown within myself, often through meditation and
visualization, where I find the ultimate treasure, the ultimate
solace: connection with my inner guidance, my sacred self.*

Grey Mist

Surrounded once again,
by a dense, ominous fog.
Hazy and opaque, a melancholic cloak,
unable to see beyond the charcoal mist.

I want to hastily wipe it with a rag,
scrub the glass of my perception:
diligently, harshly
with obsessive hands,
getting every nook and cranny.

But I resist.
I decide to—sit in it, be in it, rest in it.
A simple intention bringing a mysterious calm,
a mystic's insight,
even with the closing pressure
of the darkness surrounding me,
like a weighted blanket
with claustrophobic tendencies.

Should cause panic, right?

Strangely the fear is comforted
by the mist's somber presence,

all with the gift of unadulterated acceptance,
of true soul alignment—
of what is.

No thoughts racing to the scene
professionally trained,
prepared to rescue the wounded;
a noble cause, I suppose.

No thoughts marching forward
with the intention to attack the objective;
a familiar decisive tactical strategy.

No traversing a bit close to the whirlpool
of judgment, criticism, self-abuse,
and whatever else persistently swirls in the abyss,
until complete submersion occurs
due to the sandy banks of the mind;
a common occurrence
when you disregard the warning sign.

None of this.

Only pure, honest acceptance
of the dread contrast and its familiar, coded knock
at the mind's door, interrupting the status quo
like an unwanted, obnoxious presence

at a supposedly peaceful dinner party.
A knock, that usually triggers emotions of angst, trepidation,
instantly changing the mood of the party.

Instead,
intuitively opening the door,
cordially inviting the contrast in,
all the while holding my sacred flame vigilant
with breath, patience, trust
so the denseness now filling my home
doesn't smother the flame.

The flame always knows the darkness will clear,
providing yet another opportunity
for expansive soul growth, evolution.

I too will know once the fog fades,
skims gracefully over the hills of my soul,
grazes the meadow of my heart,
gradually dissipates into the ether of consciousness.

For now,
I am reminded to simply take heed of this pause,
an internal clearing,
nothing more, nothing less,
into the grey mist.

Grey Mist describes the internal polarity within us and how often the internal scales tend to tip toward the denser, darker part of us. The poem suggests a different way of conversating with this part of us and rebalancing the scales. For me, sometimes sitting in the discomfort, the distress, with a sense of genuine surrender and interest in my experience, helps me see it for what it is regardless of its intensity: a soul's experience. From this vantage point, I gain a view with altitude into my soul's experience, which for me allows the intensity to lessen and even dissipate while the energy moves, as described in the poem.

Mother To Mother

The energy resonating from your stance,
penetrated my being.
A sense of peace,
a gentle curiosity,
a wave of confidence and strength.

Your gaze seeped directly into my soul
attuning the chords of my heart,
as if you were conducting my soul's symphony
with this glorious hymn—
Be calm, child,
stand in your integrity and authenticity,
allow your vulnerability to move others.

The melody cascaded through me,
awakening my heart song.
Gratitude sang softly with a sense of valor
for this communion with a creature of truth,
mother to mother.

Mother To Mother was inspired by a deer I encountered during a morning run that exuded a mystical presence. I connected with her in a profound way. She spoke to my soul and provided me with the simple yet powerful message in the poem.

Willing Branches

How easy she makes it seem,
to allow her leaves to fall.
A wisdom beyond our veiled comprehension,
to release the old, to return to the whole.
In trust, she knows her bareness
will birth new life upon willing branches.

Our clutches to the old run deep:
memories, ideals, beliefs, construct our branches.
Letting our leaves fall would mean change, loss.
A burden feared with fierce determination
to flee the chance of pain.
We grasp even tighter to that which causes misery.

Who would we be,
if we allowed the expression of seasons to guide our souls?
Delightfully releasing dead leaves knowing with patience,
with trust new buds will grow into new life.
Perhaps because the new buds reside in the unknown.
We fear the transformation they will endure:
preventing new growth means no loss, right?
We grasp even tighter to that which causes misery.

How easy she makes it seem,
if only we listen to her whispers—
Let go, dear,
allow the leaves to fall
they run their course and wish to join the whole
let them be free and allow space for the new
have gratitude for the seasons of change
it is the only way to live in truth.
We release with ease that which causes misery.

Leaves commit to their journey of release,
gracefully descending with a valor of trust,
perhaps, a tear of grief accompanies their descent.

They land, rest, and wait to be transmuted into the whole.
Branches bare, free of the heaviness of dead paradigms.
In trust, knowing the bareness
will birth new life upon willing branches.

Willing Branches is about a tendency to cling to that which causes misery or holds us back. It can be old beliefs, limiting thought patterns and feelings, or longing for the past. The poem encourages us to notice the guidance and wisdom of a tree and to release the old like her fall leaves so they may return to the whole to make room and space for new life, new beginnings, expansion, and freedom. This poem speaks of my personal grief journey, the resistance to let go, holding onto what is gone, and the illumination of many disempowering beliefs. Contemplation upon how a tree gracefully endures all seasons without resistance, but with sacred knowing and trust, helped me begin releasing that which caused misery so it could be reintegrated into my soul's wholeness, and to open my heart again to new experiences.

The Soul's Hymn

Notes strategically, divinely composed upon the sheet music,
creates an espressivo blueprint of the soul.
Linear they appear,
but the music it cultivates, dances off the sheet.
Dynamic, with highs and lows, consonance, and solo beats,
waves of melody.

The music summons an embodiment of the composition:
flowing with the musical rhythm, the harmonious sounds,
feeling the vibration of the heart's chords,
allowing the music to penetrate every cell,
igniting the internal sacred flame
in a glorious symphony of soul awakening.

Each individual note intuitively touches a part of the body,
yearning for its melody.
The touch is gentle, yet profoundly deep;
a mass reverberation pulsates,
raising the soul's vibration to a higher octave.

Surrendering to the music, falling in its lows,
still supported by the hymn.
Patience, the music elevates once again.
Contrasting variances compose the soul's song

with harmony, amplitude, distinction.
Linear the notes appear, the soul's hymn transcends
even beyond the mastery of the composition.

The Soul's Hymn *was inspired by the genre of music I listen to when I'm in the process of refining my poetry. The poem describes how the music elevates my creation in such a way that the words begin to express the composition of the soul.*

Communion with the Goddess

The descent into her divine abyss
happens intuitively, no logic.
An automatic response to the nature of gravity,
pulling the weight of my body down,
sinking like a ship's anchor.

No fear accompanies the trip nor hinders the natural flow.
A journey taken often with eyes closed:
the snowy picture of the cognitive screen is turned off,
interference from competing brain waves quiets,
the curtains shut, a turn of the dial and I am within,
into another dimension.

The descent pauses, a knowing when the time is right.
Inside her core, her earthly womb is dark, quiet.
She offers suspension in an energetic pool
where safety, comfort, warmth embraces my heavy heart,
and I float upon a charged plasma of meditative bliss.
She nurtures my alignment like a developing embryo,
nestled and nourished.

The burdens I brought, dissipate.
The bricks in my shoulders, crumble.
The churning and tightening of my abdomen, release.

A feeling of weightlessness levitates,
as the waves of her kindness cleanse.
The sensation erases all prickly cumbersome worries;
I drift in a sea of compassion and rejuvenation.

Exhale deeply, she receives my gift.
A sovereign gift, often unacknowledged
for the riches and magic it holds,
any looter would seek its treasure.

The life force guiding my breath shimmers
with iridescent flecks of divine truth,
as grand as diamonds sparkling in the sun's rays.
The celestial power interwoven in each oxygen molecule
transcends beyond the reaches of the universe,
extends like a radiant wave of pure white light,
galaxy after galaxy.
She reminds me of this.

From my cue,
the ascension from her core begins
after an unknown loss of time,
she kisses the space between the brows,
the knowing eye.

A goodbye kiss with a download of ancient wisdom
tucked tightly within my soul,

an esoteric imprint, a branding of holy light,
sears my being.

A reminder of profound proportion,
of this communion with the goddess.

Communion with the Goddess describes a connection with
mother goddess (mother earth) and the alignment with the sacred
self where complete surrender, release, and solace are granted, and
ascension is gifted. This poem describes one of my sacred
meditations and visualizations.

Like Attracts Like

He didn't believe in himself,
he said,
like attracts like.

You have a strong perception of someone,
who is a ghost.

Perhaps, the ghost you're reading
is your own persona,
for the man you refer to undoubtedly
believed in himself.

Perhaps, the ghost's energy along with
the woman he accompanies
expanded so intensely in your field of consciousness,
an energy with strength, valor, integrity, receptivity
made you doubt the belief in self,
you proudly assert.

An energy you speak of possessing,
a mask you convincingly wear,
a performance you perfected.
Advertising yourself as such,
someone who can transform others
because you believe in yourself.

The woman sees your mask
and the loose strings attached,
a deep incongruent feeling
flutters in her heart.
Speaks her truth,
her truth rejected, as she suspected would be.
Like attracts like, firmly reinstated.

The woman sways briefly,
perhaps, belief in herself is fleeting
like an exotic bird facing the verge of extinction.
Yet, she knows divine truth is always present,
never lost.

Her light, although at the moment quite subtle,
has untapped power to cause an atomic explosion.
The power of fusion, where polarities
of electric, magnetic charges no longer repel the other,
but fuse into a harmonious consummation of one.

She always believed in herself,
the cobwebs of fear and doubt made her think not,
it has a tendency to override her beating, pumping heart
where sacred truth resides, finds complete solace.

Until the heart sounds off,
enough is enough!

forcing her truth, explosive light
to expel from its ventricles,
to be seen in its entirety, in glorious radiance:
shining with masculine strength and purpose,
dancing and leaping in feminine receptivity.

As you say, *like attracts like.*

Like Attracts Like *was written from deep anger over an encounter I had with a psychic medium. The poem actually evolved into profound empowerment, as I remembered who I am and who my beloved was.*

Dramatic Mask

A dramatic mask she wears, one with two faces.
A mask unknown to her, until now.
It has always been there,
she's felt the sting of inauthenticity before.
She didn't understand the dissonance at the time,
the intention is always to be loving and kind.
A role she played well;
the desire to please and shapeshift pending the ensemble,
overrides her authenticity time after time.

It is subtle this two-face mask,
almost undetectable.
The audience did not notice; the disguise entertained them.
She met their vibration, lowering any chance of conflict—
oscillating between the two sides of the mask,
an attempt to avoid disapproval
or worse to be discovered.

Pull back the curtain before her performance cue,
would unmask her authenticity—
the rawness, the edges, the curves, the corners,
the expansive space and glorious vibration
holding it all together.

Yet she knows,

her authenticity can no longer play the minor role,

no longer desires to wait backstage,

peering through the dramatic mask.

With a gentle pluck of the strings,

the mask is carefully removed, tossed behind her.

Exposed, liberated,

free of the burden to be applauded.

Dramatic Mask is about getting caught between two masks of measuring our sense of worth, our desires, our presentation to the world based on external expectations, circumstances, and relationships rather than expressing our true essence. It's about dropping the masks to align with our inner knowing and wisdom, which allows us to know and feel our true worth and not what we are told to be from the external theater. For me, I was caught between the role of pleasing others, making others feel safe and protected, rather than balancing my own needs and desires with theirs. I thought I had to dim my light, my true essence, in the process. The metaphor of the poem was inspired by my personal experience with theater when watching my daughter perform on stage.

The Story

A story created a long time ago,
by a young and pliable imagination
conditioned early to be saved by an external force.

It goes like this:
a princess encounters a terrifying, gruesome beast
drooling with a hefty appetite to swallow her whole.
Suddenly, a divine being clutching a long, gleaming sword
instantly and miraculously appears to save her.

The irony unravels decades later.
She had no idea the intensity, rugged and scaly skin,
piercing dark eyes and jagged oversized teeth,
the beast would appear.

The beast towers over her, blocking any remnants of light,
extending its claws like a medieval torture weapon.
Vulnerable, exposed,
she stands before the beast trembling,
frozen with paralyzing fear, pleading to be saved,
for someone to slash the monster into pieces.

To her dismay,
the savior would take time to be discovered.

He doesn't miraculously descend from the sky,
as once written, as once illustrated.

He's been tucked away in her mental drawers:
covered with childish things, then later with silk and lace.
Continually pushed back further and further in the drawer
at any indication of unsheathing his powerful sword.
She's not allowed to have such masculine force,
so he waits, patiently, for his invitation to emerge.

The beast antagonizes her, taunts her with its threats,
refusing to respond to the gentle, little pleas
of the good girl.
She can no longer keep the warrior, the savior,
tucked neatly away.

He wasn't external after all,
just a projected image of her own inner warrior.
At a young age he whispered in her ear
inspiring her to create this story, a prophetic message:
he will someday rise in union with her.

She summons the warrior with a prayer of readiness,
simple words laced with ancient wisdom
held deep in her subconscious.
Words with magical and majestic essence,
fused with cosmic intimacy.

The savior rises from within.
The sword drawn, held with profound strength, integrity,
swung in unison, swiftly, piercing the beast's heart.
The beast slumps, falls with a loud thump,
crushing the ground beneath it.
Its monstrous power crumbles
like a castle built with sand.

The beast smiles at her risen savior,
her divine sacred self in union,
radiating, pulsating with celestial
feminine, masculine alchemical power.
A smile of gratitude it offers
for it completed its mission with valor and honor.

A terrifying monster it brilliantly played
only to reveal the fated union;
the prophecy of a long-awaited resurrection
of the savior within.

A story created a long time ago,
by a young and pliable imagination,
only now understood,
for the virtue and fortitude, the words foretold.

The Story *was inspired by a story I wrote as a child. It was an elementary school assignment to write and illustrate a story. I came across it again when I was purging my closet. The poem uses the perspective and intention of the child story and expands it into my adult story, describing the experience of loss and pain only to regain alignment with my internal warrior self, the savior within.*

Primal Scream

You make your presence known,
once again.
A heavy mass of dense, churning fiery energy,
slowly, methodically rising ablaze
from the internal depths.

Why? Why again!

The initial impulse is to push down
with locked arms, full force,
brute strength.

Your entry brings fear.
The fear of confusion and distraction,
searching, scavenging, ravishing
through the thick brush of the mind.

An impulse to hastily clear the thicket
with a machete made of razor-sharp words,
swinging wildly, blindly, intensely.

Clear it!

The frenzy blocked, skillfully
by a pervasive energetic shield, a pause in the fight,
so clarity can beam through the chaos of the mind,
through the turbulent emotional waters
like a teleportation from another dimension.
It finds a way, with bold determination
through the mental and emotional black hole.

The clarity comes in peace,
brings suspension of time, of space,
and within the depths of the soul
a soft, faint whisper of mystic knowing
flutters forward,
landing softly upon the petals of the heart.

It is heard.

It knowingly suggests to allow the fireball
of fury, of rage to elevate.
See it for what it is—
underneath the burning, fierce flame
glows a timidness full of fear.
This flame of anger cries for help, to be seen,
the only way it knows how,
with a raging tantrum.

The whisper nudges to greet the blaze
with more than reluctance, synthetic hospitality,
but with curiosity, openness, compassion,
understanding.

It says to resist the urge to succumb
to the raw, untamed anger
with grinding teeth, clenched fists
or to be paralyzed
by the electric charge of terror,
pulsing through the highway of nerves.

Release the building tension, explosive emotion,
with a primal scream tucked deep in the soul's core,
containing ancient wisdom, transcendental power.
Expanding the soul's tectonic plates,
triggering an earthquake of release
rumbling through the physical body,
collapsing old limiting cognitive structures,
built in fear.

Allow the grains of release
to fall effortlessly through the sieve of perception.
Hold it steady,
with tenderness, with unconditional love.

No shame,
summon the primal scream,
release, rest, and be.

Primal Scream *is about anger that dwells deep within the soul*
and is often suppressed for fear of the emotion, or expressed in
untamed ways, but the poem describes a different way of
encountering the rage. For me, anger was suppressed for a very
long time. But when a tremendous loss entered my life, creating a
soul clearing, my molten core began to create fissures leading
from my subconscious to my conscious awareness. The anger
became more and more apparent as it found a way to the surface,
wanting to be seen and acknowledged. Often, I release it with a
primal scream.

A Simple Man

They smile politely,
the discomfort broadcasts across their faces.
One step to the right, edging further from your presence,
trying their best to subtly give a nonverbal cue
of their desire to escape your magnetic field.

You must be preaching—to cause such an effect.

A proud observation gallantly stands in my mind,
and now you stand before me.
Contemplation to ignore your greeting,
discomfort now overwhelms my cognitive network,
mind spinning with the reason for your interaction.
Don't preach to me, those are your beliefs,
lights up like a firefly in the web of neurons,
scurries across the synapses.

The conversation:
They busted out all the windows at the barber shop.
Who did?
Shrug, *I guess they had nothing else to do.*
That's unfortunate.
Have a good day.
You too.

Preaching was the last intention upon your lips.
Beyond the archaic structure
of the simple words spoken, a profound connection
pierced its way through the conversation,
the eyes as its gateway.
Unspoken, profoundly felt
like an invisible cord connecting our souls.

Mesmerized by the exchange, everything said
without verbal discourse,
a communion beyond the constraints of this world.

Your presence so gentle and child-like,
even though your appearance suggests
a weathered man.
A simple man you skillfully present yourself,
yet an ability to speak essence to essence,
beyond the confines of human intellect.

A truth, a simple man expertly shares,
even if not consciously.

---

*A **Simple Man** was inspired by an encounter with a stranger. The poem describes my experience with the encounter from the* *time I was observing him talking to a couple, to when he engaged me, and finally to our simple conversation. Although the conversation was basic, his eyes spoke volumes, and I had a profound experience where two souls spoke on a completely energetic level beyond my human comprehension.*

Strings

Strings guide every movement, it seems,
invisible, thinly braided, strong.
A tug on the right
creates a focused gesture of the hand,
pen to paper.

Another tug to the heart
jump starts the vital organ,
an expansive hum of energy
vibrates all around — *it's alive!*

A brisk tug upon the support string
aligns each vertebra one by one,
perfectly stacked with an architect's precision.
The alignment triggers an opening of the crown,
to receive its source.

The master of these strings
creates deliberate movements,
pulling taut, releasing with grace,
leading in various directions:
north, south, east, west,
always with the intention
of exploration, growth, connection.

Strings are attached to a gritty,
yet expansive human experience.
Strings tend to shepherd in mysterious ways,
not always translated clearly, nor accepted,
and often resisted.

Resistance births from feeling separate, alone:
a perceived inability to see who pulls the strings,
fear of the human performance.

Yet, with the many jerks
and fluid movements not far behind,
it comes to be known
resistance is part of the fun, simply a detour
for further exploration.

The path is never lost.
The master of the strings doesn't really mind
not to always be seen,
just write and you'll be fine.

Still the question begs to be answered,
who is the master of these strings,
synchronizing such inspirations?

You, my dear, the divine you.

A glance above and the strings shimmer
a silvery, iridescent sheen
with a few twinkles of diamond light,
once invisible, now seen.

Strings *is about developing a relationship with your sacred,*
divine self, which means seeing and knowing the miraculous ways
they guide your life, including both the fluid and labored
movements. It's about realizing you are not a puppet to life, but
the master of your strings. For me, as the poem suggests, one way
I connect with my sacred self is through poetry and writing,
which helps me gain altitude over my soul's experience.

The Tantrum

A physical manifestation of sacrifice, of suffering,
masking itself in a cloak of illness,
debilitating, burdensome, painful.
A unique expression summoned from its keeper's beliefs,
manifests a metastasized invasion.

Prickly, itchy, rough to the touch
awakens the sleeping keeper to remind her of its presence.
She tries desperately to ignore its persistent
nagging, tugging, pulling,
an agitated assertion of pain,
sharp stinging sensations, relentless itching.
She's dragged to meet the suffering in its physical form,
engaging in anything to relieve its tantrum
only to exacerbate its symptoms into a spiral of misery.

Amidst its screaming and yelling,
a belief appears sharply and clearly in the keeper's mind
like a flamed torch illuminating a dark cave.
A belief of having to sacrifice, to suffer,
in order to receive.

An ancient belief, so it feels,
possibly originating from several lifetimes

leads to a familiar stabbing, piercing of the heart:
all for the greater good,
the same sacrifice time after time.

Perhaps bringing light to this hidden belief of the dark,
a creature of nostalgic proportions,
will calm its flailing and boisterous expression
and release the attachment to a belief in sacrifice, in suffering.

For the tantrum was thrown as a dramatic ending
to a deeply anchored paradigm,
as intense, severe, painful as its beginning.
No longer serving the keeper's transcending beliefs,
nor her rising divine feminine power of receiving.

Within the warmth of her sacral,
in the depths of her beating heart,
resides a nurturing, welcoming space to receive—
unconditionally,
without suffering, without sacrifice.

The Tantrum describes a physical ailment that caused suffering. As I wrote about the suffering, I received an ability to see beyond its physical manifestation and to see its essence, where I found a deep-rooted belief: I had to suffer, I had to sacrifice, in order to receive. Freedom begins with awareness.

Solar Eclipse

Golden rays of warm luster, hues of purity and divinity,
cascade down with glistening icicles of light.
Penetrates the barriers, patiently waits to be received
not in passing, not in complacency.

A subtle nudge to posture towards this glorious source,
open the energetic gateways to receive divine solar energy.
Holy rays of mystical dimensions
touch, then fuse into the essence of the soul,
spinning and intertwining like a synchronized dance.

A fluid alchemy of two sacred elements
cause a glorious reaction of igniting and illuminating
every immaculate particle of the body,
as bright as the sun's rays,
cell by cell.
A grand production forcing ascension,
radiating the highest expression, the highest potential.

An aura bursting with rays of celestial origins
surrounds the finished masterpiece,
anchored with a golden beam of light
of pure magic and mysticism.

Illuminates the crown with a glorious halo,
drives its energy through the body, to the feet into the earth.
Thrusting the host back, opening the sacred heart
into a climactic posture of ultimate reception.
A complete union of soul and spirit,
a return to all that is.

Solar Eclipse is about receiving the sun's energy on a cosmic level where it activates your solar body, creating a powerful internal alignment and a clear channel from Heaven to Earth. This poem describes another one of my sacred meditations and visualizations.

Walking with Lack

You have been a companion for so long,
my loyal friend draped in foe robes.
Lack is the name you go by.
We know each other quite well,
walking together along life's path many turns of the wheel.

A path negotiating, at times skipping alongside,
the mind's subjective, reality's objective landscapes:
battlefields sweating the blood of turbulent emotions,
meadows exhaling the fragrance of sweet love and wild lust,
hot desert land showcasing mirages of mental illusions,
dense forests filled with towering trees of hope and freedom,
harsh concrete plagued with the energy of anxiety and fear,
majestic peaks communing with crisp, clear thought.

All of which varied in proportion, dimension, density,
time after time,
but the attachment to you remained the same.

I've come to realize,
you provide a false sense of protection—

Four walls to support a conditioned way of life, a cyclic life,
constantly, desperately seeking to fill the potholes

left by the weathered belief in you,
my friend, my foe, *Lack*.

Perceptual windows looking upon the society
that values you most.
A society slow to change,
thriving on the fear and sadness you tend to exude
across the collective consciousness,
like a rolling dense fog causing extreme low visibility.

And a glass ceiling to cap any extravagant expansion
or sovereign way of life.

Although, without your knowing,
Expansion and her lover, *Freedom*, slipped their way in
teaching a different way of relating, of communing.

They visited often, as the door was left unlocked.
Each visit we became stronger, grander,
swelling with potential, a new way of life,
pregnant with clear vision.
Belief in abundance and prosperity as a birthright.
Outgrowing the compression from the walls surrounding us,
the consistent, steady pressure from your relentless hold,
until a breakthrough.

It scared you, it threatened your control.

You tried to reinforce the walls with studs made of fear,
seal the cracks with doubt.

Your efforts although futile were honorable,
desperately trying to stop any change to our normal.
The clarity of your presence, your purpose
has been seen, has been accepted.

Don't worry about your position or your role,
without you, the fullness of love, expansion, freedom,
would not be known.

My sweet companion, it's time to loosen your grip,
to allow your opposite to walk side by side.

Love, draped in fine linens of abundance,
jewels of prosperity,
will no longer navigate in your shadows,
waiting to be seen.

Dear *Lack*, you don't have to leave—
you just need to know,
you are not the only one walking this path.

Walking with Lack is about the journey with a belief in lack, and how this belief can distort perception and disrupt peace and harmony from within. This is a belief that has been a long-standing companion for me. The poem describes the rebalancing of the internal scales due to self-awareness, exploration, compassion, and connection with my inner wisdom, my sacred self.

The Tapestry

Woven tightly with precise craftsmanship,
across the concept of time,
lies your experience and my experience.
A tapestry enlaced with past images, obscure memories,
complex designs of a nebulous future.

The present is rarely the theme of this fine tapestry.
Typically hidden, woven behind the persistence of past motifs
or the chase of future scenes.
A technique taught generation to generation.

Even with the traditional ways,
it only takes one weaver to focus intently upon the loom,
shining their brightness of clarity upon the tapestry's potential,
remembering a weaver always has a choice in their art.

With new threads of elevated content,
the weaver envisions a different tapestry motif.
Weaving with no fear of the past or future,
feeling the threads glide with ease and grace
into an intricate, clarity guided design,
seeing the loom poetically weave an enlightened experience,
one of truth and divine intercession.

They remember weaving is full of enchantment,
is actually fun.
With each stroke of the thread
and little to no attachment to the images appearing,
just simple delight in the experience
of weaving one's life.

The Tapestry *describes the contemplation of my relationship*
with life, which quickly seemed to use the metaphor of a tapestry
and the weaving process. The use of the metaphor helped to
remind me that I have a choice in how I relate to life, to remember
the magic in the soul's experience, and to have fun along the way.

The Cavern

Deep in her internal cavern
where she rises from the depths,
then settles in the darkness,
is quiet, still, expansive
like an infinite lake of pristine consciousness.
Here she is not seen, observed, judged.

She holds her space with ease, a graceful fluid dance,
a deep knowing of her intricate, yet simple essence.
Clarity with a keen sharpness, esoteric truth,
expands like a sound wave vibrating through
both her interior and exterior atmospheres.

She communes with the rhythm of mother goddess,
oscillating between the warmth and coolness
without restriction or judgment of the subtle contrast.

Even with this profound, safe space,
she desires to be seen, to experience more contrast.
Not just a little contrast, but a substantial amount:
a heavy dose of critique, confusion, fog.

Her wish granted, her manifestation unfolds
and she rises through the cracks of crystallized perception.

Not forcing her way through, but finding the least resistance,
until she emerges into soft, porous fertile soil
of the external reality,
expanding her glory into a nearby river of potential.

She relaxes in the flow of the rippling waters,
allowing it to carry her, hold her,
flowing with the changes in the current:
from raging rapids to stillness,
cyclic death and rebirth.

Colliding with mental blockages,
bumping into emotional rocks along the way.
Bruises and cuts mark her soul,
the cost
to negotiate such collisions.

Still, she perceives abrupt shifts in the current
as only opportunities to grow, to expand.
Gaining discernment when to be still
and when to be fluid.
Always rejuvenated, replenished,
upon communion with her deep, dark cavern,
the core of her origin.

The Cavern is about the journey within, into the darkest, most hidden part of you. Within that sacred space, safety and support is found, until the knowing and the desire to be seen again urges you to resurface and integrate your inner wisdom into the external reality. The poem describes another one of my meditations where I again commune with my sacred self and mother goddess (mother earth).

Merry-Go-Round

Hello worry, how you sprang forward once again,
like a jack-in-the-box taunting me to indulge
in your endless game,
ride on your merry-go-round.

I did hop on,
spinning round and round, a few revolutions,
asking to go faster and faster,
until the turning of my stomach awakened me to the torture,
that was masked by seemingly innocent fun—
the false sense of control I believe you provided
and thought to be so "fun."

The pillar of truth grounded in the core of my being,
refuses to spin no more.
Choice.
To dig my foot into the sand of peace surrounding your ride,
stop the persistent momentum of limiting storylines,
anchored in thick, mucky fear
and to halt the merry-go-round of relentless
thoughts of lack.

At first, the stillness
brought a subtle queasiness of resistance:

Who am I without my beloved worry?

I don't know yet,
but experiencing inspired thoughts aligned
in stillness, in love,
embracing my heart's expansive desires,
rather than succumbing to the centrifugal force of fear,
is worth finding out.
No more,
round and round we go.

---

*Merry-Go-Round describes the cyclic addiction to worry and
mental stress, yet choosing to shift the focus from the chaotic
mind to the heart, and with practice gaining a sense of freedom
from fear and worry. I rode this merry-go-round since I was a
young girl, where worry seemed to plant its weeds in my young
mind, only to be overgrown in my adult mind, causing a sense of
mental and physical suffocation and exhaustion. I had to do
something about it, so I began to clear the weeds to make space for
new growth and expansion to be nurtured and nourished.*

The Ride

I've traveled across several mountain ranges
in two decades time, from one to the other,
it's where my heart finds solace, protection, inspiration.

Mountains seem to always provide a gateway to her,
where I commune with her
in her grandest, most confident gown.
My bias of course, mother goddess, as I refer to her,
mother earth, known by others.
She embodies an immaculate fusion
of feminine, masculine energy
always opening herself, so I may seek respite in her core.

I left a quaint, whimsical home sitting snug among her pines,
firmly built in the foothills of her red peaks.
One of fae notoriety, one of enchanted fantasies.
Bewildered by the logical, analytical reason for my departure,
yet this nebulous state of mind triggered inspiration
to write the verses, the heartbeat of the words now unfolding.
A tug of my intuitive reins, a knowing it was time to go.

I rode this stallion before,
trust braided in the reins,
intuition voiced the commands.

I returned to the original peaks after a long, arduous journey
of many ironies, paradoxes, revelations.
A story worth telling as it manifests into poem,
perhaps even a chant.

It began with the original peaks,
often gazed upon in the impressionable days of youth.
A time of quiet, studious, revered contemplation,
seeking knowledge, seeking truth.

The peaks witnessed the darkest and lightest moments
of the early times, even an initial spark of awakening
from a deep human slumber.
Always providing a nurturing, maternal embrace
through it all; it wasn't enough to stay, though.
I was a young blossoming woman needing to ride elsewhere,
to seek expansive growth and love
and to endure its harsh contrast.
So I left, many years ago, vowing not to return.
A tug of my intuitive reins, a knowing it was time to go.

I rode this stallion before,
trust braided in the reins,
intuition voiced the commands.

It wasn't long before the peaks summoned my return.
Battle-ridden, the stallion returned with a slow, tired gait,
a bittersweet homecoming.
Devastating heartbreak, raw, jagged emotional pain
loaded upon the saddle.
An abrupt, sharp clearing of the soul,
a tower crumbling to its knees.
The dreaded fear manifested;
my beloved killed in a political war,
leaving me behind to raise a divine gift of life.
I answered her call though and returned to her peaks,
to once again gaze upon her majestic stance.
Her rugged presence shows physical evidence of being risen
from a volatile, turbulent past event,
like me, like my little one, like her.
She stands with strength, empowerment,
with patches of fertile green growth in her jagged edges.
We stayed for a while heeding her guidance,
resting in her solace,
until our new footings were firmly set, but not anchored.
A tug of my intuitive reins, a knowing it was time to go.

I rode this stallion before,
trust braided in the reins,
intuition voiced the commands.

The ride was different,
drawn to the vast flowing waters of her deep sea.
No peaks in sight, just thick forest of tall emerald pines,
all leading to the edge of her waters.
We grew, we struggled,
experienced the sharpness of contrast,
just as her waves showed us, the continuous ebb and flow,
death and rebirth.
Her vast ocean often offered baptismal cleansings
of our evolving souls,
breaking free from old fears, limiting beliefs.
Learning to take our first steps in a new world,
a new way of perceiving, but we couldn't stay long.
A tug of my intuitive reins, a knowing it was time to go.

I rode this stallion before,
trust braided in the reins,
intuition voiced the commands.

We were led to the red peaks,
where the whimsical, pixie home stood.
A new world stirring, churning the energy of my sacral,
creative, fluid flow of energy rising and expanding
into my heart
in ways, in sensations, I've forgotten.
An energy I neatly tucked away for safekeeping,
but no longer desired to be hidden from full sight,

from full consumption.
Bold choices and decisions presided,
promising the potential of complete fulfillment,
expansion into a higher dimension.

My little one too expanded and retracted in new ways
of knowing, of believing.
Opening her sacred eye, healing her tender heart,
digging her mote,
a safeguard from potential energetic vampires.
We couldn't stay long,
to ground this creative surge among her red peaks.
A tug of our intuitive reins, a knowing it was time to go.

I rode this stallion before,
trust braided in the reins,
intuition voiced the commands.

Back to the original peaks,
where it all began, we returned as higher vibrational souls.
Brushing off the last few lint and dust balls,
mottled with fear that still cling to our awakened garb.
The stallion now roams freely among the foothills
of her majestic, rugged stance.

A feeling I may be here awhile, perhaps a time to commit,
as I prepare the young blossoming woman,
I've raised with all my heart and soul to ride elsewhere,
to seek expansive growth and love
and to endure its harsh contrast.

She knows how to ride the stallion,
trust braided in the reins,
intuition voices the commands.

I love you Rhea, beyond the reaches of the Universe.

The Ride *is so incredibly special to me. It is about both the internal and external journey, pilgrimage, and adventures of my daughter and me. It includes deep loss, growth and renewal, and soul expansion. It describes my connection with mother goddess (mother earth), with whom I always find solace, strength, and renewal.*

Poem

It doesn't have to be a poem:
just let it flow
allow the words to surface
emerge with insightful momentum
without resistance, judgment, filtration
open the heart's levee
drop the mental chains
break the glass of fear
channel the messages
no hindrance, no doubts, no critique
dance in the intensity of the poem's beat
feel the vibration caressing the soul
articulate its divine frequency
expand with the evolution of words
feel the electricity through the spine
the tingling across the chest
the enticement to open the heart
further and further
open, rise, expand.

Poem *is mostly an unedited session of automatic writing. All the poems in this collection originate from automatic writing where I just put pen to paper and write with no censorship from my mind and heart. The words flow from my soul. I later refine the writings into free-verse poems.*

The Purge

It rose with a purpose,
like a brewing, smoldering volcano
preparing for its grand burst of glorious release.
First, came the intense ejection of smoke,
the prelude to ultimate expulsion
of anger, sadness, limitation.

I urged your burst with a chant.
Simple lyrics dwelling in the depths of my shadowy core,
where molten rock churns in lack,
boils in a pool of self-defeating beliefs.
I chanted the forbidden word: *die, die, die.*

Don't be alarmed,
I have enough altitude now
to know this chanting of death, of anticipated ending
is meant for the attachment to fear, doubt, lack.
Simply an abrupt energetic shift of the old ways,
so the new,
may flow with passion and grace.

Elements of a bound self needing an explosion
to shatter it into pieces.
A blast so powerful it incinerates

the lower aspects into fine dust,
drifting upon ribbons of enlightened wind.

I do not hate these parts of me,
I used to.
They bound me in tight ropes, sometimes heavy chains,
far too long.
I dragged this weighted, clunky burden time after time.
I know this because of its familiarity,
a persistent, dull undertone.

Such attachments need a little more force
to release its talons,
its deep clutches in the human experience
than just good intentions of love and light.

It needs a dramatic event to be liberated,
a substantial clearing of the energetic field,
to allow the reunion, the realignment
of the sovereign self.
Freedom of old limitations, cognitive blocks,
opening the channel so the mystical waters of the soul
flow
with a consistent, unhindered wave of abundance, prosperity.

For unprecedented clarity, calm, silence,
to follow such a glorious release,
and write the epilogue to an epic soul cleansing,
to begin the next chapter with hawk vision,
and a robust heart.

The Purge *describes the purging of the mind and heart, of allowing the burdens, self-defeating thoughts and emotions, and the sense of lack to surface, where it meets an empowered internal boundary. The boundary is established to not allow such entrapment to dominate. I found in the process of my internal work that I've uncovered so much of this, and like an inquisitive archaeologist, I kept digging, not to torture myself, but to truly understand the workings of my mind and heart. From the dig, I found compassion and unconditional love for all of me: the dark, the light, the feminine, and the masculine.*

Why Wait?

Oh dear, you are shedding.
Is it a natural process?
Shedding an old skin, like a serpent's epilogue.

Or are you dying?

The colors you expose are warm, calm, mesmerizing,
bold and intriguing.
Emerald green with splashes of yellow,
the color of wheat fields,
glistens through peeling bark, the color of rust.
Rust doesn't quite give enough splendor; I'll try this again.
Bark, a deep red hue perfectly highlighted
with vibrant orange tones,
as if an artist had her way with you.
A keen smoothness presents under the rough, textured bark,
appears to be the work of a mystical carpenter's tool
revealing an intricate and harmonious fusion of contrast.
Your aesthetic boldly projects from the gray, wet,
cold background.

Oh dear, I hope you are not dying.
Your beauty is extraordinarily unique,
authentic and divine.

Regardless of your process, I am in awe of your presence,
an ability to expose such colors and grandeur of fae notoriety.

How I wish to unclothe my truth,
with such brilliant stature as you—
to show off pending change, possible exit,
with a celebration of earthy, enchanting colors,
textures of divine symmetry and harmonious contrast.
Worthy of any goddess's court.

Why wait?
pierces through the state of reverence
with penetrating firmness and crystal clarity,
as if the message came directly from you.

Why wait?
A simple phrase, two words suspend in the psyche,
the only words present within a void of thought.
Words energized with an abundance
of electric charge and magnetic force,
holding the same beauty and divine presence as you,
vibrating with an irresistible frequency
of strength and knowing.

I answer—
with the same simplicity, the same power.

Yes,
Why wait.

Why Wait? *was inspired by a tree outside of a coffee shop. Her beauty, strength, and uniqueness spoke to me deeply, and she provided me with a powerful reminder. A message to shed whatever is holding me back from exposing and then expressing my most authentic, radiant, divine self.*

Diamond Light

A diamond was given to me in a dream,
not any old diamond,
but one of mammoth proportions
suspended in an esoteric dimension
of another world.

Rotating slowly with precision and harmony
magical, mystical,
twinkling with laser specks of light,
hues of pinks, blues, golds.

Each speck exploding with its own glory
like fireworks in a black, moonless sky.
The grand finale,
the diamond bursts with an awe inspiring
white and gold light,
beams of divine light, radiating far and wide.
A star of its own.

But to my horror,
the rays push back a dense, black darkness
to expose a demonic wolf-like creature
with metal claws and fangs,

stiff, brown leather-like fur, red devilish eyes,
lurking in the shadows.
A shrill of terror charges through my veins
as the creature comes clearer into my vision.

The diamond light offers protection,
strength in my core, fortitude in my spine.
I offer an intention to this creature of the night—
*may the diamond light transmute your energy
into holy light and unconditional love,
if you so wish.*

To my astonishment, the activation worked;
the horrifying metaphoric symbol of raw fear,
fades and dissipates
into the bright luminous light,
dissolving the nightmare into nothingness
and its power over me.

My response, *what a gift!*
A weapon of transmutation, even transcendence,
is now nestled in my heart.
A diamond's majestic presence
and explosive power, crystalline strength,
emanating intuitive rays of love and compassion,
all for me.

A gift invoking a spear of empowerment,
a cognitive sword of clarity and divine simplicity:
nothing else matters.

All troubles, confusion from the mental,
material dimension flutter away
and my focus is transfixed
upon the sparkling, rotating gem of clarity,
chiseled with expert craftsmanship
of sacred geometry,
vibrating a cosmic hum
beyond detection of the human ear.

Always at the ready, my diamond light,
to expand its energy of pure divinity,
protection, star potential,
upon my call.

---

*Diamond Light describes a dream. I dream vividly and now
know my dreams are a way of tapping into other dimensions, of
diving even deeper into my soul and processing the workings of
my mind and heart. This poem describes one of my dreams, and
my experience with receiving a divine gift of light, only for it to
help me clearly see my darkness, which presented itself in a*

terrifying form. This diamond light gave me the strength, both in a dream state and in waking state, to relate to my darkness with less fear by offering an opportunity for transmutation and transcendence.

Clouds of Enchantment

Tired, with a touch of anger, a heavy dose of agitation,
drapes over my existence.
A familiar experience of dread enters,
but something feels different.
Is there a tinge of enchantment,
cleverly disguised as angst
mingling with this familiar visitor?

A revelation appears with the masquerade,
I'm tired of being everyone else, but myself.
The comparison between my authentic self
and who you want me to be,
creates a fierce competition in my mind.
Who to be?

The chaotic internal shape-shifting to please you,
runs deep like thick, tangled roots penetrating the earth.
Anchored in the mind's many layers
of hardened thoughts, beliefs,
of blatant resistance to change the internal dialogue
for fear you won't like me.

It makes my body ache, my shoulders throb.
I feel restricted,

with prickly, anxiety-filled energy pushing against
the cage containing it.
A cage constructed from false identities:
all to please the other,
perhaps inherited, taught, or just contrived.

Like a magician's trick,
the draw to compare then compete is so tantalizing,
convincing, yet boringly familiar.
The temptation alluring, to wade in a pool of misery
for it is known so well—
fumbling around in a condensed, unsatisfied,
material driven world,
a world constantly seeking truth in faulty external promises,
all the while mutating self to keep up with the demand.

Compare, compete,
survival tools to feel recognized, to feel accepted, to feel loved.

Enough!
I say to the whole prisoner paradigm,
disempowered mentality, trapped by my own thoughts.
It is I, who stands before you.

It is enchantment, after all:
unique, talented, radiant,
thriving in my essence of softness, of warmth,

of feminine power that was often held back
by misguided masculine armor.

My metal breast plate, sword at the ready,
dominated for some time,
fiercely protected an essence as delicate and transforming,
as drifting clouds with glowing, golden edges
for fear these clouds of enchantment would not be accepted.
But the armor hindered expression
of my authentic, sacred self,
often blurred the path, causing frequent detours,
finding myself in taverns of comparison,
drinking spirits spiked with inauthenticity, unrequited love.

This righteous armor is no longer needed
for the possessive protection it gallantly offered.
I know I created you.
You played the mental tape as long as I needed,
as I desired.
I pushed stop and then eject, a new tape inserted.
I'm ready.

It is enchantment, after all:
as the clouds of my essence
merge into form, transcendental form,
with spontaneous shifts of vapor
held not by untamed, overprotective masculine force,

but by an expansive masculine presence.

A presence reaching far and wide,
offering a safe space for unyielding soul bloom and
expansion.

All for my enjoyment, pleasure, bliss,
complete permission, support, and protection
to undress my most authentic, sacred self.

Not for anyone else, but for me,
no comparison, no competition.
It is so,
I am who I AM.

---

*Clouds of Enchantment is about the temptation to compare the
authentic self with who others want you to be, leading to an
internal competition between the two which causes a chaotic
shape-shifting to please others. The frantic shape-shifting is an
effort to be seen and acknowledged according to an external's
expectations. All of which leads to a deep sense of
disempowerment, even fear or confusion of your own truth, your
sacred self. The poem describes a calming of the shape-shifting by
the rebalancing of the divine masculine and feminine within*

(mind and heart) to realign with the sacred self. The realignment is an empowerment anchored in ultimate truth allowing the soul to freely express its authenticity. I know the role of the people pleaser, the over giver, and the harsh judgment of self that follows these roles quite well. I played the part for a long time so much so that when my canvas was cleared, I wasn't sure what made me happy, what made me feel safe, what I desired, or what I dreamed to be. This was even more convoluted with harsh self-judgment of not feeling worthy enough for my dreams to manifest or to express my highest potential. Until now.

I Understand

What is it like to move in that body?
A body that is slow, unstable, wobbly:
poorly maintained, poorly fueled,
trying to find energy from the little will—to live.

You remind me of someone.

When I see you, I feel the conflict
between needing help and shooing it away
with quick little thrusts of the hand.

I feel the sadness,
how did it come to this?

Sure I'm to blame, as you might say,
but I'm too tired to care now.
I desire to stick around for you, my family,
but this old vessel I inhabit
is rusty, rickety, desires rest.

Every so often, I'm teased
with surges of energy, I know are fleeting.
It almost makes this old vehicle
run a little bit slower,

knowing when this weary engine
decides to stop,
a complete relief
awaits me on the other side.

It's hard to savor these good times,
knowing it will move along
as quickly as clouds on a windy day.
I'm afraid I've already dug my grave.
I now stand between the earthen walls.

It's only a matter of time,
before I decide to exit.
I'm no longer at a place to heal, to revive.

I'm at peace.
I would love to see you at peace,
rather than the sympathetic expressions
upon your saddened faces.
The sorrow you exude,
the disapproval mixed with a cup of anger,
a pinch of resentment finishes the recipe.

I know it hurts,
even angers you to see me this way.
It is what it is,
as I've said to you, time after time.

I don't want to change.

I wish you would respect my decision,
to leave this tattered, run-down vessel,
to be free of its inabilities, limitations, old parts.
Let's honor my exit,
not to stay.

I understand, Dad.
I love you.

I Understand *describes my perception of my father's suffering and his failing body before he passed. The poem was written after his passing, but I feel I may have channeled him while writing it. The verses in italics represent his voice. He provided me with another way of perceiving his transition, which gave me such comfort and release during my grief.*

It Depends

Reviewing the mental battle,
strategies taken, mistakes made.
A battle most wouldn't understand:
she only gave you a compliment.

The battle began as it often does
by a frequent taunt, an arrow of judgment,
or perhaps purely a benevolent compliment:
I wouldn't have guessed your age, you look so young.

The canon fires and the mental conflict begins.
The typical loss of words of how to respond
to a seemingly innocent, perhaps even,
complimentary sentiment.
Usually, it annoys the hell out of me,
and I
fume inside with scattered, agitated thoughts,
colliding and repelling like excited atoms:
How can you think I'm still in my twenties?

So much life has happened since my twenties,
widowed, single mother, four career changes,
despair, growth, anger,
expansion, restriction, liberation.

Life—I've negotiated so much life
and you think I'm still in my twenties!

There are times though, I actually
accept their judgment as a compliment.
It must be my young genes,
I say or sometimes add,
it must be my fairy blood.

Oh I got it, it's a blessing,
to appear not to age, perhaps it really is
other-worldly, mystical, a cosmic gift—
a divine goddess essence
exuding an unforgettable presence.
I like this,
it all depends how I want to experience it.

A simple declaration, yet profoundly cathartic,
charged with exuberant power, enlightenment,
broadcasts across the mental radio waves.
Grants immediate detachment
from the familiar pressure, the mental scramble,
of how to respond to the perceived judgmental attack.

The after-action review concludes
with deep contemplation of the cognitive dissonance.
The conflict, the contrast within,

reconciling utter discomfort with actual contentment:
it all depends how I want to experience it.

What a relief, as clarity appears out of nowhere.
The battle wasn't fought in vain after all.
It all depends, shines brightly
like sudden headlights upon a foggy road.
It is true, growth is fleeting without contrast.

With this new blessed clarity,
I don't judge the experience one way or another,
battle or no battle,
it's just that—
the experience my soul desired.

It Depends *is about feeling small and not feeling seen or honored for*
your wisdom and strength. For me, my conflict with looking young,
which most people wouldn't be bothered by, was a continual trigger
for feeling discounted or overlooked—of not being taken seriously,
and of naivety. Even though I look young, I've experienced so much
in my life and gained so much invaluable wisdom that I often feel
closer to someone in their later years. The poem magically reminds
me it's all about how I perceive it, hence "it depends," and a
reminder to lighten up, to not take myself so damn seriously, and to

enjoy the youth! The poem references some military terms, which is based on my past military experience.

Stay Put

A heavy, thick cloak burdens
my shoulders once again, shortening my stance,
by at least two inches.

It drags along the ground with each step,
slowing my pace
and immediately transports my mental state
into another reality of
gloom, depression, fog, confusion.

A reality at times, I have difficulty leaving,
perhaps because I can't see the exit
or I want to stay,
because it's familiar.

Heavy, thick, consuming cloak,
each step forward is a lifetime journey.
I know wearing this weighted garb
only holds me back.

Dragging, tugging, straining,
so much effort to just be content, satisfied.
Exhausted, my eyes droop,
despair, fatigue settles in.

Would sleep offer some relief?

Pulling, shuffling, hearing
the haunting sound of the cloak
as it roughly skims the floor.
I'm in it,
succumbed to its weight
to my knees, head down,
surrender, rest,
stop forcing, stop resisting.

Everything melts, dripping to the floor,
tension releases, emotions cascade
forming a pool before me.
The thoughts, oh the thoughts,
after a long tedious, poorly strategized battle,
finally surrender.

All that is left is a lavish void
of complete surreal silence.
A sea of quiet, expands and traverses
beyond the edges of the mind,
stretching beyond the confines of the body.

Relaxing, nurturing, tender catch and release.
Each inhale brings more calm and serenity,
each exhale extends

the etheric body further and further,
stretching stiff, rigid bones, muscles,
consciousness.

The confusion recedes,
and reveals a profound crispness, clarity,
oneness.

I stay put, right where I am.
Fully, genuinely present in this shift of perspective,
so it may seep into my veins,
infuse into my marrow,
charge my neural networks,
jump start my sacred heart,
transmute my energetic field.

In this space of total refuge,
I stay put, right where I am.

---

*Stay Put describes the burden of deep dissatisfaction, of lack, of
depression, and how this burden slows life to such a dreadful pace.
Rather than trying to relentlessly do something about it, either to
be rid of it or become more dependent of it, the poem describes a
different way: by truly surrendering and resting in the darkness.*

The poem speaks of my experience with this heavy cloak, where I was able to find peace and solace by allowing myself to be in it without judgment or hate. The experience helped me to perceive the darkness in a different way, as if the darkness just wanted to be seen without an agenda, which was enough in this experience for it to shift and move, providing me relief and clarity.

Muddy Waters

Murky, thick waters of a dark stagnant pond,
full of restricting beliefs and thoughts
coalescing to form a heavy, thick soup of resistance,
of "I cant's."

One step in this pond takes so much effort,
as the muscles strain to push
against a barricade of intense fear,
of preconditioned mental mud and grime:
trying to make me continue to believe
what I truly desire
is impossible.

Effort, extreme effort exerted
to just put one foot in front of the other.
Wounds from the past obscure any clarity.
I can't even see my feet,
intense opposition to move forward.

All this mental effort to just take one step forward,
almost succumbing to hopelessness,
summons panic and paralysis.
The uncompromising fear, to live another way,
hovers over me, capping any expansion.

This fear doesn't protect me as it cleverly promises,
but provides false reasoning
to justify my current state of mental overexertion
and no movement.

If I'm not careful,
I just may let these viscous, opaque waters
of suffocating, raw resistance
to swallow me whole.

Yes indeed, something has to change.
I don't have enough reserves to continue as I am,
pushing against the dark, muddy waters.
So I write.

Words allowed to flow effortlessly,
a stark contrast to the current internal condition,
even creates a surge of clarity, a crystal-clear emotional purge.

Words gaining momentum like a geyser
releasing the pressure, the mental stress,
showering over my dark state of being,
flushing through the dark, murky, muddy waters
until I surrender, loosen the internal viscosity
and flow fluidly, freely,
creating a whirlpool of harmonious contrast:
clear and opaque waters

allowed to swirl, intermingle, merge into each other,
as one.

A new energy finds its way beneath my feet,
pushing upward, so I release the resistance, the fear.
I choose to lay my head back, raise my torso,
expose my chest, open my heart,
and float upon the waters of inner duality—
rest, surrender, breathe,
finally flowing with the current of the soul.

Muddy Waters describes the feeling of entrapment, of feeling bound and restrained, paralyzed by fear, where any movement forward feels almost impossible. For me, I was able to move by writing, and the writing simultaneously helped to energetically release the bonds that entrapped my mind and heart.

The Good Girl

I do what I'm told, and I receive.
I receive love from you, so I believed.

Love? I interpreted it as love,
with my young developing heart.
I know it was your intention of love.
As you always wanted what was best for me,
as long as it was what you wanted,
as long as I was doing what I was told,
it was best for me —
the good girl.

No offense as I bring this up now,
as you are no longer playing in this realm.
I know you've already transcended this plane.
I feel it in the depths of my heart, your liberated soul.

I'm still here though, playing in this realm,
not quite as transcended as you
that's why I bring this up now.
So I can be free of the constraints of this belief:
I only receive love when I satisfy other's desires
for me, for them,

and I do what is expected of me—
the good girl.

But I'm not doing what I'm told now,
ironically,
I feel more of your support than ever before,
a gift of divine transcendence.

---

*The Good Girl describes how I internalized part of my
upbringing, which followed me into my adult life and manifested
in various ways, with the same core belief, of being "the good
girl." This poem is about the dismantling of the deep-rooted belief
and allowing all of me to be present, not just the good girl.*

The Scout

You are coming.

I feel your energetic resonance close to me,
as if you sent a scout to give me a message
of your future arrival.
A scout to conduct a reconnaissance,
if the risk of contacting me will be worthwhile.

I feel your energetic presence,
the immense strength, a boulder of confidence.
A presence so grounded and replenishing,
it nourishes my emotional soil,
caresses the valley of my heart.

I see your smile,
a perfect bow placed upon the gift of your energy.
An energy washing warmth and ease over me,
like a steamy shower of expansive love
and acceptance.

I am consumed by your smile,
a smile so powerful it penetrates my heart chambers
with a reverberating love wave of immense amplitude.

A wave of complete safety, of tender frequencies,
an esoteric embrace of the highest resonance.

A magical spell you sent with this scout.
A spell that is perfectly aligned, harmonized,
both magnetic and electric
attunes my internal rhythm with a deep, low chord,
invites the vibration of my heart to integrate
and resonate with yours,
carrying a love sound
beyond the reaches of the universe.

A love that melts me,
as the magnetic pull to surrender
causes all tension and burdens
keeping the muscles of my soul taut,
to drip to my feet in a pool of release:
a complete opening of the divine feminine.

The electric charge your scout brought
pulses through me from the sacral to crown:
aligning every vertebra,
straightening my etheric posture,
opening the womb of creation
until the final stature of confidence, radiance
is risen
and the sacred heart blazes.

The way your energy integrates with mine
is profound, familiar, runs deep, other worldly,
a sacred home.

I send a message with your scout—
I'm ready,
when you're ready,
it's been worth the wait.

The Scout is about divine, sacred love of glorious reciprocity, and support; of a deep, sacred connection and a feeling of home. It describes my sacred partner on his way to my heart. The poem uses some military references and terms based on my military experience.

Phoenix

I'm not doing enough,
lurks in the darkness,
in the most hidden corners of the mind.

A constant presence, a reliable undertone.
It shows itself often, usually when it's quiet,
when there's not much going on,
but space, time passing,
as I watch an external world
running on a hamster wheel.

A familiar response, quite a loyal thought:
If nothing is happening outside of me,
then I sure in the hell
will make something happen,
inside my head.

And it begins, endless ruminating,
a constant prickly buzz of worry, anxiety.
So critical, so damn judgmental,
of how I'm supposed to utilize my time,
this time,
when nothing is happening out there.

An effort to scavenge for control;
I suppose,
to see into the unknown.
Ironically, even with this chaotic mind,
I feel the yin to the yang.

Even beyond the dominance of fear,
I feel abundance, prosperity, opulence,
way beyond my wildest dreams.

The feeling overwhelms my internal world,
even tames the agitated lion prowling in my head.
A feeling that leads to a deep knowing.

A knowing all hopes and dreams
are just a smidgen past the horizon of fruition.
A knowing of pursuing a silly dream,
is already true.
How do I explain that to you?

It's not you, it's me.

I owe the explanation to
the little girl who always dreamt big,
but her dreams were dampened,
soured, put on hold,
because it didn't meet their dreams for her.

She learned to put it aside, cover it up.
She was busy being everything,
for everyone else.
Her deepest desires, soul potential, infinite creativity,
left unfulfilled.
Abandoned by self-sacrifice, the need to please,
to transmute the energy drawn to her
for that's the dependence of those around her.

Not anymore, my little one, we're dreaming big!
Your desires dancing in my heart are felt.
All of them out there including this adult critic,
can go to hell.

What I mean, they can figure out how
to release their own bondages,
take care of their own discomfort,
step out of their own hell,
all by themselves.
It ends now.
I am doing enough.
We are enough.

Step out of the smoldering fire,
our time in hell is done.
The phoenix is risen and blazes free.

Phoenix is about feeling as if you are not enough for your family, for society, for the world, for yourself, and the anxiety and fear that typically accompanies this belief. The poem describes my response to this belief, causing extreme mental stress, and my investigation into the pulse of these thoughts, where I found the backstory to the self-defeating belief, which created compassion for the self. And from this awareness, an internal, energetic boundary was set in order to restore empowerment.

The Queen is In

I am ready
to receive my beloved.
A sacred, internal rebirth
to fill my cups with divine light
of total rejuvenation,
of ascension proportions.

Much has been purged, cleansed,
all for your arrival.
The door is unlocked,
please come in
and take me.
My heart is wide open
for you, for me.

The way is clear now
and I receive what is mine,
by divine birthright.

It comes in
way bigger, grander,
than I could ever imagine
or hoped.

Bold, deliberate, expansive,
so tender, intimate
yet driven, energized
with a deep cosmic knowing,
infused with the sweet aroma
of fresh acceptance.

I reclaim my domain,
alert my court
with a pound of my staff
to send a clear message,
exuding an etheric shock wave—
the queen is in.

The Queen is In pays homage to the sacred self and the receiving of all of your divinity after the space has been prepared for the union of the mind and heart, the divine masculine and feminine within. For me, this homage has been a long and arduous journey, but worth every step.

Rooms to Clean

How long do I wait for you?

A promised reward
for diligently exploring
the many rooms of human conditioning.
Rooms that appear to be endless,
in this mansion of consciousness.

Every turn leads to a new hallway,
doors, and more doors, so many rooms,
to clear, clean, dust, sweep.
Finishing the whole cleaning escapade
with the aroma of a sweet, yet bold feminine scent
that enlightens the musty, stale odor
of old, outdated beliefs.

I'm getting tired though, room after room,
I've diligently cleaned.
I've been such a loyal attendant,
arriving on time, dust cloth at hand,
always ready to work.

Sometimes doing my work with ease and grace,
with curiosity and anticipation

that tends to pirouette in my sacral:
knowing the many sacred mysteries awaiting
behind each of the solid doors,
knowing the exquisite clothing, treasures to be found
in the many ornate closets.

Often, or at least it seems,
I drag my feet along the dusty floor
for fear the disappointments
will outweigh the happiness I seek.
My patience dwindles and I pick up the step
to hurry up and get the job done,
get to the end,
get to the outcome already!

Often, or at least it seems,
I'm attracted to the same closet with the usual contents:
a heavy, dark bleak cloak
that I routinely drape over my shoulders,
feet drag even slower with each weighted step;
a soft, gray veil adorned in intricate lace
placed upon my crown, falling precisely over my eyes
to shroud my vision with such purpose and precision.
A stupendous, yet ominous outfit
distorting time and perception,
doesn't disappoint.
It feels like an eternity when wearing this costume,

the waiting, the preparing,
for you.

Just drop it, take it off
the cloak, the veil, the illusion,
and discover
time is the same,
there's been no eternity of waiting,
no time loss, no delay,
no snag in the cosmic fabric of possibilities.

No matter how often I put this damn costume on,
all experiences are worth the wait.
No matter the grittiness, the dirt, chaos filling the rooms,
all experiences are worth the knowing.

It's all a part of the whole cosmic expedition,
a desire to grow, change, elevate,
contract and expand,
to breathe the essence of creation,
exhale the desire to be set free.

When you do arrive,
after all rooms have been inspected
some cleaned, some left alone;
I'll see you clearly.
This time,

no cloak, no veil, no disguise,
but absolute naked truth.

Hallways seem to magically disappear,
doors vanish, the mirage dissipates.
A wide-open space remains,
radiating your warmth and the soft glow of your torch.
The space seems to breathe:
billowing with abundance, possibilities,
oneness, greatness.

All is finally revealed, unveiled,
you are here.
Of course, you have always been here,
but that was part of the mastery, even the pain
to find you, to know you.
It turns out,
I needed the journey in its absolute entirety,
in order to feel the exquisite wholeness of my sacred self,
to feel the ultimate truth, from within.

Rooms to Clean *is about the diligent internal work of exploring your mind, heart, and soul, only to discover an absolute magic from within. This poem describes my personal internal journey, the cleaning and preparing, the pain and discomfort, the exploration and discoveries, and the union with my sacred self.*

Cobwebs

These cobwebs of disappointment, of fear,
are real,
sticky to the touch, difficult to shake off.
Clearing the webs brings a creepy vibe,
chills of the unknown crawl their way up the spine.
Only for the webs to return,
time after time.

Why do you,
Fear,
make such intricate designs weaved with seduction,
temptation to fall victim to your traps?
Why do you entrance your prey
with pretty, iridescent shimmers from your silken threads,
promising a source of light into the dark, scary caverns
of the unknown?
Why do you capture innocent creatures
such as opulent, auspicious beliefs,
beliefs in happiness, success, love, warmth?

Suppose you have to feed too,
but you tend to trap too much—
hoarding your meals, meals left uneaten.

Your webs are out of control
strung in every corner of the mind,
even in the ventricles of the heart.
These threads obscure hope, trust, faith
from crystal clear vision, authentic gratitude.

There are so many cobwebs
entangled with deception, illusion, delusions.
And I let you have full reign of this domain,
to cast your webs far and wide
across the peaks of consciousness
and even impress upon,
the fertile valleys of the subconscious.

It's time to clean it up,
rein in your alluring, labyrinth of traps.
You have plenty of food.
You have plenty to eat.

Cobwebs *describes a relationship with fear, the dance with fear,*
until balance is regained by establishing a firm internal boundary.
As the poem describes, using the metaphor of a spider and its
abandoned cobwebs, fear has a purpose, but it doesn't have to
control us. For me, fear has often entangled my experience with

the unnecessary stickiness of mental cobwebs, until I acknowledged its purpose, its desire to keep me safe, even in false ways, could I appreciate its presence but also give it some loving house rules.

Material Things

I like material things, I collect like a raven,
attracted to shiny objects.
I know why I do what I do, or at least I think so:
to fill the gaping hole that longing creates,
while waiting for my miracles to manifest.

Is this why, truly why, I collect?
What else do these items provide me?

Instant pleasure, reward:
if it's not happening fast enough in the external,
then I'll buy my own rewards, pleasures, treasures.
Once again, to fill the mammoth hole
that longing dug and hazardously left.

Is this why, truly why I collect?
What else do these items provide me?

I like nice things, to be aesthetically pleased,
it lifts my soul to be adorned
in fancy, shiny, well-functioning, high quality things.

Is this why, truly why I collect?
What else do these items provide me?

I deserve it,
to have the ability to obtain what I desire,
to feel abundant, opulent, affluent.
Frankly, I deserve to be abundant, opulent, affluent
in all aspects of my life.
I know damn well the external is not the source of this,
but it is a part of it, isn't it?
I know the internal workings of the mind and the heart
projects itself on the movie screen of our exterior lives.

But what if we help the interior self
by offering external treasures?

I like material things,
they are simply the ornaments to my soul's holiday tree.
I don't need to shame it or feel guilty
for my desires,
for even obtaining these material things,
sometimes hastily, impulsively
and
sometimes patiently, strategically.

I'm the one who fuels the power within these material things,
whether I enjoy them or feel guilty for having them.
The soul continues to grow, contract, and expand,
through all experiences with the material thing.

It's not really about the material things,
but the life I breathe into them.

Material Things speaks of the attachment to material things and the dissonance it often creates. This poem explores my own attachment to material things only to find a truth in my experience that resolves my personal dissonance. I realized the power I place upon the attachment, all attachments, is the flame that ignites the type of experience to be had.

Find Me

In the shadowy, dark sediment of the human experience,
you will find me.

In the nutrient filled roots nestled deep
in the silky mental mud,
you will find me.

In the solid, yet timid stem trusting its fate
to find its way to the surface,
having the faith to spread its emerald leaves
upon still, inviting waters of the expansive heart,
you will find me.

In the knowing when the time is right,
to unfold and extend delicate petals
of vibrant color and variation,
to birth an exquisite, infinite, spirit filled lotus self,
you will find me.

In the crystal-clear essence of endless potential,
in the solar rays of the sacred self,
in the sovereign soul of gratitude,
you will find me.

You will find the time spent in darkness,
submerged in the womb of creation
is absolutely vital for complete and authentic,
bloom into light.

Find Me uses the metaphor of a lotus flower and its life cycle to describe a soul's cycle, knowing I will always find the sacred self, the divine self, during my own cycle. The poem is about the journey into my soul's darkness and the ascension into my light.

Something Feels Different

Something feels different,
a new state of being, a new foundation.
It feels as though I finally found the exit
in a maze of dark, obscure conscious beliefs and feelings,
including all the hidden corners of the subconscious.
Even reached the peak of a mountain
raised from earthquakes of disempowering conditioning.
The climb, a bit arduous, grueling at times,
but worth the effort,
even with all the pain, doubt, and trepidation.

Something feels different,
all the work, digging deep into the depths
of the heart, of the mind,
all the meddling in the formation and workings of beliefs,
all the diving in the vast sea of emotions,
all the diligence in exploring the intricacies of the soul—
has not been a waste of time,
has not been in vain,
but has invited inverted truths to the surface,
to be seen, to be acknowledged, to be released.

Something feels different,
an immense sense of relief

as burdens and mental stress wash away
under a fountain of illumination,
under waters of liberation,
igniting a soul freedom, promising a mystical celebration.
There's even an acknowledgment of how far I've come
in this internal journey of deep exploration,
where endings continue to cycle
and all life begins.

Such mastery gained along the way.
Yes, I can say mastery,
I have nearly mastered the self
and exalted the sacred self.

Something feels different,
all my heart's desires unfolding
in the most miraculous ways,
in perfect order,
and with open realization.
How truly fortunate I am,
the expansion is profound—
radiating like a heavenly star in the night sky,
openly receiving golden treasures,
flowing with the ripples of life,
and swimming at last
with the current of the soul.

Something feels different, for sure,
the union of the heart and mind is here.

Something Feels Different is about as the poem says: Something feels different. Although ALL that I desire hasn't manifested in physical form, the internal transformation and the union of my heart and mind, the divine feminine and masculine within, has been and continues to be a profound journey. The journey is providing a soul expansion beyond the reaches of the universe.

The Cry*

I want to transcend
become the water
that rages and swells.
An uncontrolled ocean
never to be tamed.

I want to transcend
become the storm
conjuring the wind
that feels like daggers.
Feel the surge of lighting
and hurl it through the sky.

How powerful would voices be now
silenced by my rushing waves
and screaming thunder.

I want to be a force of nature,
more than I already am.

—RJ Pintor

*A poem written by an absolute divine gift to me,
my daughter.

About the Author

Stacy L. Pintor is a poet, writer, soul coach, and a mystic. She believes in poetry as a powerful healing, therapeutic, and transcendental tool for relating to life's challenges and transitions. Stacy is a former military officer and civil-environmental engineer, and a former licensed clinical social worker. Visit her website, baresoulworks.com, which includes a blog that offers soul-healing practices and examples of how to implement them. *Alchemy of the Soul* is her second collection of poetry. Her first book of poetry, *Into the Darkness, Become the Light*, was published in 2016.

BARE SOUL LLC
Poetry and Soul Healing

baresoulworks.com

Magic is within and all around you. Believe in You.
Love, Stacy

About the Publisher

Glass Spider Publishing was founded in 2016 by writer Vince Font to help independent and self-published authors reach readers through professionally edited and artfully designed books. The company is headquartered in Ogden, Utah, but has published authors throughout the world including the United States, Canada, England, Kenya, South Korea, and Vietnam.

GLASS
SPIDER
PUBLISHING

www.glassspiderpublishing.com

www.ingramcontent.com/pod-product-compliance
Lightning Source LLC
Chambersburg PA
CBHW031423120626
46545CB00006B/2244